The Weeping Angel Prediction

Michael X Barton (Author)
Alfred Steber (Editor)

Saucerian Publisher
Original Sources in Ufology

© 2025, Saucerian Publisher
All Rights Reserved

ISBN: 978-1-955087-68-1

All rights reserved. No part of this publication maybe reproduced, translate, store in a retrieval system, or transmitted in any form or by any means, electronic, mechanical, photocopying, recording or otherwise, without prior written permission from the publisher.

THIS is an Educational and Inspirational Monograph especially written and intended for NEW- AGE individuals everywhere. It contains Seven fascinating chapters. Statements in this Monograph are based on Scientific and Super - Sensory findings . No claim is made as to what the information cited might do in any given case, and the Publishers assume no obligation for the opinions expressed or implied herein .

 # Foreword

The mere fact that an Angel in a picture in a place called Worthing, England, developed an odd habit of "weeping" , is not too important in itself.

True, it is a phenomenon. And phenomena serve a useful purpose in attracting our attention and arousing our curiosity . But the real purpose and value of phenomena usually is behind the manifestation itself . So it is with the Weeping Angel .

A nameless Supernormal Being , who simply tells us that he is the Truth, the Light, the All throughout the Universe, is the power behind this phenomenon. It is he who is responsible for the weeping of an angel in a picture in Worthing . And it is he who also caused the same type of manifestation to take place recently in Hollywood , California.

He apparently is using this unique phenomenon as a " sign" to draw our attention to his presence and power and most important, to his PLAN for humanity .

"Without a vision , the people perish , " is an old saying and a true one. Just as true is the recognition that -- lacking a plan -- the noblest ideal or vision cannot be manifested in our world.

"THIS IS MY PLAN, WHICH IS ABSOLUTE."

With the publication of this Monograph, New Age students in all parts of the world will become familiar with this being as well as with his plan.

The unbelieving will scoff at these things; the weak in faith will doubt them, but TRUTH is indeed stranger than fiction, and such manifestations will increase in number and in power spread from continent to continent 00 until the living Spirit of Truth is recognized by all.
--MICHAEL

IN GRATEFUL ACKNOWLEDGEMENT

The Master - the Cosmic Visitor who is responsible for the phenomenon of the Weeping Angel picture and other manifestations of a supernormal nature, all of which are calling Man's attention to his prediction of a sooncoming event of much greater significance.

Richard Grave - the "ordinary sort of chap with an ordinary sort of job" whose startling contact with the Master in April of 1961 resulted in a most extraordinary sequence of events.

Liebie Pugh - of the Universal Link, in England. Her inspiring service in documenting the basic facts of this story, was of the utmost value to me in writing this Monograph.

Katherine Hayward - whose personal experience is reported herein and who is the representative for The Universal Link in Hollywood, California.

Anthony Brooke - the world traveller and practical "messenger of light" who first called my attention to the "Weeping Angel" episode and its implications.

For
Having made this Monograph possible.
-       THE AUTHOR

CHAPTER 1
What is it All About ?

It all started happening on April 11, 1961. The outer phase, that is. And it happened to Richard Grave in a locality known as Worthing, England.

Richard Grave is an ordinary family man whose job is selling real estate. The photo at the bottom of this page shows Mr. Grave holding in his hands a picture which, because of the remarkable phenomenon connected with it, has come to be known as " The Weeping Angel " picture. (Photo from The Reading Chronicle.)

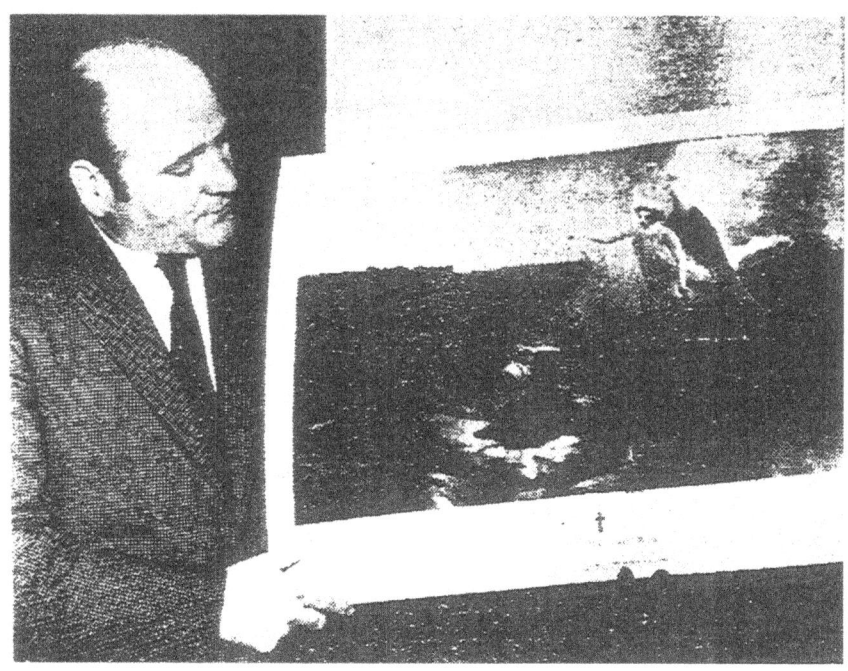

But to begin our story, I must first tell you what happened to Richard Grave in 1961. Richard had just moved into a new house in Worthing, and was clearing out some rubbish in the garage next to the house. There he found an old Victorian Print 8- an oleograph -- covered by glass, in a frame 18" by 24" (approx.) Without bothering to examine the picture, which he simply regarded as rubbish left by the previous occupant of the house, Richard Grave placed the picture under his right arm and started walking toward the trashbin to throw it away.

Suddenly, a most astonishing thing happened. A Supernormal being, apparently from another dimension, appeared in front of Richard, blocking his way. "I AM HE", said the Cosmic Visitor, as he reached out his left hand and touched the picture. The glass on the picture shattered into bits and the figure of the Mysterious Being disappeared in a blaze

of orange light. So intense was this light, Richard Grave thrust his left arm upward to shield his eyes, and his forearm was immediately burned.

Greatly upset, Mr. Grave carried the picture into the house, set it upon a side table, and put a dressing on the burned arm. A half hour later, Richard Grave's wife came home after having visited the hairdresser. She took a look at the picture. It was dark, badly blistered, and only fit for the trash can. They put the picture down on the floor, to be disposed of later.

About an hour later, Mrs. Grave looked at the picture once more. Immediately, she called out to her husband, "My God, look at the picture!" Richard also looked and saw, to his complete amazement, that the picture was no longer dark, but of a clear colour and the blisters were gone. It was as if some unseen hand had worked to perfectly restore the picture.

Looking closely at the picture, they noticed that it was a scene showing the Angels announcing the coming of Christ to the shepherds, entitled " The First Christmas Morn".

Mr. Grave had hoped that all of this was only some sort of hallucination, a temporary upset that would soon be over with. He and his wife had even laughed at his original fright when the picture -glass was first shattered by the " visitor ". But on seeing the picture restored, his fears of the unknown began to return. Something very peculiar was going on.

<u>On Wednesday, April 12th, (1961)</u> the mysterious figure made another dramatic appearance. It happened like this: - The picture had been placed in a different room and was lying face upwards on top of a trunk. During the course of the day, Richard Grave had occasion to enter the room where the picture was. As he opened the door, he saw something quite incredible.

There, hovering above the picture, was the same figure he had encountered in such a startling manner the day before! Mr. Grave was terrified. Slamming shut the door, he dashed through the house to find his wife, who, when she went into the room with him, could see nothing except the restored picture. She could not see the figure hovering above it. But that figure was still there and -- it was plainly VISIBLE to Richard!

<u>On Friday April 14th</u> Mrs. Grave noticed a patch of water forming on the floor where the picture stood. She told Richard about it and he took it out to the fireplace to dry it. Then they realized that the water was coming from the face of the foremost angel in the picture. It was "weeping". This flow of water continued in spite of the fact that the picture was left in front of the fire for several hours.

To test how much water was flowing from the picture, they placed a plastic pail under

it . In two days the pail was filled to the brim . Other persons were called in to witness the " weeping " of the angel in the picture and they also saw it weep and even tasted the water . It was salty . Intermittently the weeping continued; sometimes only a few drops appeared and at other times it would weep for hours. A number of witnesses are willing to sign sworn affidavits attesting to the fact that -- in their actual presence -- the amazing picture " wept" . Soon the "Weeping Angel " story was written up in the Psychic News.

<u>On May 4th, 1961</u> a woman of deep spiritual insight and keen mentality , by the name of Liebie Pugh , saw the article which appeared in the Psychic News, concerning the picture and the strange visitor who had been appearing to Richard Grave.

That very night Liebie Pugh wrote to Mr. Grave, asking for permission to visit him . She received permission by return mail , and on May 6th paid her first visit to his home. From that point on, Liebie Pugh sensing the vast importance of Richard's amazing contact -- began keeping a written account of all phases of the phenomenon , including each contact he has had with the Cosmic Visitor . These " visits " with the Being who Richard refers to as the "Master" , number over 6,000 so far .

During these visits -- which last anywhere from 15 minutes to several hours on occasion -- the Master dictates messages or instructions to Richard , who in turn types them after first checking them with the Master and then hands them to Liebie Pugh for general distribution .

According to Liebie, Richard Grave is a man of character and integrity . He is sincere beyond any question , and has an entirely practical approach to life . You will be interested in knowing also, that he has no " religious " background or experience, and this being who appears to him and makes these tremendous statements says nothing which need connect him or his plan in any way with any religion of any kind . Nor does he attempt to "convert" anyone to anything .

Rather he tells people to follow only what is truth to them till they be ready for the next step in their unfoldment, which is inevitable, of course, since we are all "awakening " . Also, this Cosmic Visitor urges all persons to stay with and follow only what reflects LOVE and TRUTH to them . He does not relate his "plan" to this little earth or to earth's humanity especially . It is always the <u>universe</u> he refers to.

In August 1963, Liebie Pugh put down on paper her personal observations and conclusions as of that date. Here is what she wrote in her newsletter, quote:

"The question is often asked, 'What is it all about ? '

"It is about a fact. That fact is that a Supernormal Being, who tells us that he is the Truth, the Light , the All throughout the Universe, has been appearing, walking , talking on this

earth since April, 1961.

"His appearance is as solid and normal as anyone's and his voice is equally normal. He appears at present only to Richard Grave, whom he

calls his instrument. To Richard he dictates what he wishes us to know and Richard takes the words down on a typewriter and hands them to me for distribution.

"By this method this Being eliminates the interference of any human mind and he names his contact with us the NEW DIRECT LINK. His sojourn with us has been accompanied by numerous wonders which appear to be given to us as evidence of the unique power of the Being operating among us."

Though he only appears in this objective form at present to Richard Grave, he is seen and heard in many ways by many people. Without giving any date, he has stated that he will have revealed himself to the Universe by Christmas 1967 through the medium of nuclear evolution.

"That is the outward picture of what is taking place. It was suggested that I might add to this outline my idea of what it's all about inwardly -- fundamentally. This led to the following brief attempt at clarifying my thoughts on the matter.

"I would say, fundamentally, it's about the imminent winding-up, or ending of what can most easily be called the UNIVERSAL ILLUSION and the imminent REVELATION of what underlies this illusion. Perhaps it would be well to stop just there, as that is all that can be factually said in my opinion ... " L.P.

More than 75 direct messages -- of unusual interest -- have been given to Richard Grave by the " visitor " since April of 1961. Although not all of the Visitor's statements will appear in this Monograph, I shall include a large number of them at opportune moments, so that you will be able to study them and also feel the POWER of them. :
1. I have created the divinity within the picture.
2. I have given unto the Universe many manifestations of my presence this century.
3. I am the Son of God - nothing is manifest except through me.
4. Follow your own reasoning in the knowledge that the Father understands ALL.
5. Take heed of me and know me fully.
6. There are many who are aware of my presence among them. They can do nothing to enhance my full manifestation except hold faith and proceed in their own light until I am ready.
7. By the first second of the first hour of the seventh Christmas morn hence I will have revealed myself to the universe through nuclear evolution.
8. I am most satisfied with my earth link to whom I shall make my very being known in

certain manner, leaving nothing to their imagination and so ensure a satisfactory conduction of the NEW DIRECT VIBRATIONS now going out throughout the Universe .

9.There will be many and more substantial manifestations to follow so that the prophesy of my coming may remain kindled.

10. Pay no regard to those who question you and profess their skepticism . They will know of your experience through the medium of other , greater revelations and so they will seek you out in reconciliation .

11. Ensure that my scribe is ready and informed of your impressions so that a documentary may be completed at an early date - the inspiration will be from the divine as always .

12. The link necessary for the completion of my coming to the Universe is vast and rather complex in its make- up. Those involved are being moved. Be prepared for surprises in the composition and the evidence they will be required to produce .

13. To effect my materialization I require many instruments and this will create, to an extent, confusion; much deliberation is therefore necessary among my true followers so that they may tread wisely.

"The Master "
(from a sculptured model by Liebie Pugh.)

"Walk in my light and in my knowledge."

"Remain with what reflects truth and love to you throughout, until I am ready."

HOW TO MEDITATE UPON " THE WEEPING ANGEL PICTURE"

Included with this book you a beautiful reproduction of The Weeping Angel Picture . It shows the Angel of the Lord appearing to the shepherds in the field and announcing the birth of Christ .

We recommend that you hold the picture in both hands, while gazing upon it for 3 minutes or longer , each night just before you go to sleep . It is also a splendid idea to have the picture near your bedside so that you can see it easily in the morning on awakening . <u>Any unusual manifestations</u> should be carefully and accurately noted at the time they occur . For this purpose, a notebook and pen should be kept handy, near your bed.

CHAPTER 2
I Meet Anthony Brooke

It was while visiting my good friend Gabriel Green in Los Angeles during March, 1963, that I came into the "orbit" of Mr. Anthony Brooke. I had just been ushered into Gabriel's house by Gabriel himself, and was preparing to diseuss some important matters relating to the New Age and "UFO's" or Unidentified Flying Objects.

Suddenly I became aware of another man, a guest in Gabriel's home. He was a tall, distinguished looking gentleman with a quiet self-assured manner. I got the impression that he was a man of strong purpose, and that this meeting was not -- as it seemed on the surface -- just accidental, but that it was a part of a thrilling Cosmic Plan now working out on earth. He spoke quickly, using precisely clipped words with a definite English accent.

"How do you do? My name in Anthony Brooke, " he said. Then, without beating around the bush, he came directly to the point . " So you are Michael, " he continued, "What can you tell me about flying saucers ? Have you had contacts with any space beings? "

I shook Anthony Brooke's hand, and although we had never met before, I sensed an inner kinship with him. I frankly was impressed by his refreshing directness, and his enthusiasm. The average " man in the street" has a scoffing attitude towards unknown things, especially such things as "flying saucers" and space people from other worlds.

I have had such contacts, " I admitted, "though I seldom mention these matters any more except to close friends who are open-minded on the subject. There has been a great deal of misunderstanding in regard to the reality and mission of the space people, and those who had courage enough to openly tell about their 'UFO experiences ' haven't had an easy time of it."

Mr. Brooke agreed, and I invited him to attend some of my "New-Age Lectures" which I held each week on Friday evenings in Los Angeles. The meetings were held in a small church hall, and there I spoke freely on all phases of higher unfoldment. It was a Wednesday when I first met Anthony Brooke at Mr. Green's home and I looked forward with a joyous anticipation to the pleasure of seeing him again.

That Friday at 8:00 P.M., I was pleasantly surprised to see Anthony Brooke waiting for me at the little church where my New Age class lecture was to be given. After a cordial

greeting at the door, he went in and sat down among the other members of the class and waited for me to begin my talk.

I told of my various experiences in realms beyond the ordinary; of how I first became awakened to the possibility of beings who are not of this earth; of my own contacts with such beings; and of the tremendous significance of the Biblical verses from Matthew 13: 38&39, which read as follows:

"The field is the world; the good seed are the children of the kingdom; but the tares are the children of the wicked one. The enemy that sowed them is the devil; the harvest is the end of the world; and the reapers are the angels."

After the class meeting was over, Anthony Brooke and I arranged to have lunch the following afternoon at Albert Allen's Restaurant in Hollywood. He told me how much he enjoyed my talk the previous evening and during the course of our conversation I learned more about the remarkable Mr. Brooke.

THE WHITE RAJAH

Mr. Anthony Brooke is a direct descendant of Sir James Brooke, who in 1841 became known as the first "White Rajah" of Sarawak, an Asian land in northern Borneo. Three generations of Mr. Brooke's family ruled this country of Sarawak as an independent state for just over a hundred years. The last Rajah before the country became a British colony in 1946 was Mr. Brooke's uncle, Sir Charles Vyner Brooke. But Mr. Anthony Brooke himself ruled the country for a time with full powers. This was at the time of the outbreak of war with Germany in 1939, when he signed the Proclamation as Rajah Muda.

"You know," said Anthony, while we continued our interesting conversation at the restaurant, "I quite agree with you and of course with good Saint Matthew, that a separation of good seed from the tares, wheat from the chaff, is occurring. No doubt this takes place more dramatically at the close of every Age."

"Yes," I commented, "the phrase Matthew used: 'at the end of the world', really means the end of an Age. At such a time -- and in my own judgment we - are definitely living in that end-time now -- a cosmic change takes place within our universe which causes a destruction of most of the outworn, obsolete material values in our world. Those things no longer seem so important to us. New, spiritual values and ideals take their place. Naturally, such ideals can be terribly upsetting to a great many people who are still clinging to the old values."

Anthony slowly nodded his head and sipped some tea. The next words he spoke were destined to plunge me into a totally unexpected New Age adventure, which was to prove to be one of the most thrilling experiences of my career."

Michael, have you heard of the Weeping Angel ? "

I confessed that I hadn't. With that, Anthony Brooke graciously filled me in on all the details of the phenomena which had been taking place in England since April , 1961 when the Cosmic Visitor first revealed himself to Richard Grave .

Why I asked the following question I honestly don't know; but like the man said after he had jumped into a patch of prickly cactus, " It seemed like a good idea at the time! " . What I asked Anthony was this , "What quantity of tears do you think the angel in the picture has wept since 1961? "

The answer I got was, "Several bucketfulls!

"Turning my attention more directly to Anthony , I expressed an honest desire to know more about him and his work.

"Yes," he replied, "In 1946, when the British Government and my uncle Sir Charles Vyner Brooke, decided to make Sarawak a British colony without consulting the wishes of the people , I opposed the move on the ground that it was illegal and unconstitutional, and furthermore , that the people of Sarawak had in no way been consulted. For five years I campaigned against the unfair decision and as a result was exiled from the territory .

"Happily, in August, 1963, Sarawak became a member of the new Federation of Malaysia and it is now ruled by a Malay Governor. The ban on my entry has now been lifted , though I no longer have any political connection with the country .

"I decided to devote my life to world travel to help promote international understanding and peace. I speak Esperanto and use it to address people who do not understand English , for I find it helpful in creating a new feeling of oneness among men.

"In my travels I have visited many countries in Europe, including the Scandinavian countries. I visited Russia, Poland, Hungary , Czechoslovakia , Jugoslavia and also the Middle East, India, Pakistan and Asia . In India I walked from village to village for a week with Vinoba Bhave. I have talked with Pandit Nehru in India, and with Chou En Lai in China."

Anthony Brooke paused momentarily . His teacup was empty . So was mine . I ordered another round of tea. "

No doubt you have contacted a number of New Age groups , " I said, " Do you feel that they are talking about essentially the same things such as coming world changes , various

kinds of strange phenomena , the Weeping Angel with the prediction , flying saucers , and a new spiritual awareness ?"

"Indeed, " Anthony responded , "there seems to be a common ground upon which all of these groups all over the world, are beginning to meet more strongly than ever before. I would agree that this new common ground seems to be a spiritual one a new and more vital awareness , one might say. One notices an unusually dynamic force, spiritual in essence, working in all of the different groups . Since 1958 a definite 'upbeat' appears to have been added to individuals and members of all groups. This new impetus is decidedly spiritual , in my opinion , and it seems to be sweeping through the entire world -- now. "

"This Weeping Angel episode," I remarked, "Just how does it fit into the larger scene of what is happening everywhere?

"Humanity, " replied Anthony , "is experiencing what can only be called 'spiritual break-thru' on all levels. Everyone , be he butcher, baker, candlestick- maker or whatever area of human service he be laboring in, is waking up to a tremendous fact. This fact I refer to is being thrust, so to speak , right into our midst by unseen but nonetheless terrifically real , universal forces . It can no longer be ignored ."

"What is that fact ? " I inquired."

This . That the manifestation of the Real World is imminent. A Day of Revelation of what some may choose to call the 4th- Dimension, is almost upon us. The Weeping Angel phenomenon is a sign -- and not the only sign -- now being given to humanity , to awaken us to the all - covering fact that the One who is presenting these phenomena (and who claims to be Truth itself) is also telling us something else . He is notifying us those of us who will listen -- that by 1967 he will have <u>revealed himself to the universe</u> through a process he terms nuclear evolution."

CHAPTER 3
Angels -- Why They Cry

It was a quiet afternoon in Los Angeles . A full year had hurtled by with almost express-train speed since my luncheon with Anthony Brooke, world- traveller extraordinary . Shortly after our last visit together , he had returned to England . I looked idly at my calendar . It reported the simple facts that the day was <u>Saturday, February 8</u> , But somehow I sensed that this would turn out to be an eventful day . Just how eventful I was soon to discover .

Strangely enough, my mind was full of thoughts of Anthony . I wondered if our paths would ever cross again . No doubt he was about his chosen work, on a lecture tour sc.neAlbert where . It could be anywhere , of course, for Allen's Anthony Brooke's New Age activity was global . And -- for all I know -- it might even be Coffee Shop classed as "universal ".

No matter . If Destiny so decreed, we'd meet again . Till that happy time my mind would cherish fond memories of him, for I had liked Anthony from the start , and admired him for his inspiring presence and ideals.

Musing thusly , I reached for a sheet of paper to place in my typewriter . As I did so, my eyes were drawn magnetically -- it seemed at the time -- to the window nearest me. I glanced out to the street. The tall , dynamic figure of a man carrying an important - looking leather briefcase , was striding toward my house. I pushed aside the window curtains and looked again .

"There he IS ! " . I shouted enthusiastically so that my wife, Violet, came rushing from another room to see what on earth was causing all the commotion .

"Anthony Brooke is at the door ! " I explained , and the two of us ran to fling the door wide open, and to welcome him back to the famous " City of the Angels " . We celebrated our happy reunion by lunching at our favorite restaurant -- Albert Allen's -- again. Joyously we compared notes on the latest developments in the Universal Link activity , the Weeping Angel phenomenon, and most recent instructions from the Cosmic Visitor who was appearing to Richard Grave.

"The Universal Link is growing, " said Anthony, "We have received this word from the

Visitor via Richard Grave. He tells us also that TIME is of little consequence now. " (Note: I have gone more deeply into this phase in another Monograph entitled, "Time No More",-- Michael) "Did he elaborate on that idea ? " asked Violet . "Yes, " Anthony replied , "I think the exact words he used were: 'As night approaches, day may never come instead the light will pour forth from my Father's House. '"'

"That may come as a SHOCK to many persons ," I remarked.

"Possibly," admitted Anthony , "However, in another message received by Richard, the Master has stated: 'There can be no real surprises - all must go according to plan without any exception whatsoever .

"Is the picture in Richard's house still weeping ?" asked Violet.

Anthony nodded in the affirmative. "Indeed. There seems to be a fantastic force operating to produce that phenomenon. Many more persons have now seen it . The picture still weeps . But there are other facets of this amazing story I have not told you before, and they are interesting."

The noise level at Albert Allen's was at its peak , for it was lunchtime and the luncheon crowd was still pouring into the restaurant and the crosscurrents of many different conversations fell on our ears from all directions .

"If they only knew what we were discussing , " I said jokingly to both Anthony and Violet, "I wonderhow they would react?"

It did seem rather ludricrous . Here we were talking about strange and miraculous things -- angels , pictures that cry real tears, prophetic things to come, etc. 80 while the people all around us were apparently interested only in mundane affairs.

"No need to lower our voices , " Anthony said, " Even if anyone should overhear our conversation, which is doubtful because it is taking place on an entirely different level, they wouldn't be able to make heads or tails of it anyway! "

I asked whether or not anyone seeing the angel in the picture actually weep, was curious as to WHY it did so.

"Some yes, some no, " was the reply . One could quite easily read into the phenomenon many "reasons" as to why the angel was crying . For example , although many are called, so few are chosen (because of their stubborn " ego " and little self-will) that it truly is a "crying shame" . Or, perhaps the angel is crying because the time of Divine Judgment is now upon all men, and the severity of some of the judgments will be so great that the minds of men will be hard-pressed to understand. " For then shall be great tribulation,

such as was not since the beginning of the world to this time, no, nor ever shall be." -- Matt. 24: 21 .

Still , the real reason may be far more obvious . It may be simply that the Cosmic Visitor who now is appearing quite objectively to Richard Grave is drawing attention to himself and his Spiritual Plan , by means of the Weeping Angel phenomena .

"Mr. Grave has a pet bird, a Budgerigar (Australian parakeet) named Joey , " said Anthony Brooke. "One day the Master -- the Cosmic visitor -- opened the bird cage and the bird became aware of his presence. Joey attempted to alight on the Master's shoulders and the Master increased the solidity of his figure sufficiently to enable the bird to perch securely upon his shoulders. Now that Joey is acquainted with the Master, he allows the Master to lift him out of the cage whenever the Master wishes to do so.

This is quite amusing to Mr. Grave's little daughter Carol , who enjoys immensely watching the bird perching on an "invisible " figure , apparently suspended in "mid- air" without support!

We were delighted to hear this, for it clearly showed that the Master has a very solid form and occupies a very definite area of space. It at once debunks any notions one might have as to any merely <u>visionary or imaginary</u> nature of this Being .

"Has Richard described the Master ? " Violet asked .

"Yes, he has. After he lost his original fear he began to feel quite joyous and elated, and during the thousands of visits with the Master , Richard Grave took notice of numerous details. He describes the Master as very youthful looking , the face rather slim , without a moustache. He has a rather sparse beard, rather high cheekbones, and his eyes are blue-grey . "

At this point Anthony interjected the earliest conversation that Liebie Pugh had with Mr. Grave on this topic . I quote:
L .: Does he smile ?
R.G. No, he is serious. He seems only interested in what he wants me to do, and seeing that I get on with it . L .: Well , does he attract you so that you like being with him?
R.G .: (Thought a bit and said) I can only say that it is as if you are in love.
L .: You couldn't say anything more expressive .
R.G .: He gives an enormous sense of power and of drawing me -- nothing hypnotic , not the least like that, but a tremendous drawing towards him . (end of quote).

We paused briefly in our conversation to order some of Albert Allen's world-famous cheese- cake for dessert. Then the subject of angels and angelic ministry came up.

"Frankly , " I confessed, " this entire episode of the Weeping Angel picture has rekindled in me a great interest in angels . And some of the conclusions I've come to are quite

astounding."

"I'll agree with you, Michael," said Anthony, "that angels have a definite and highly important role to play in this end-time drama now going on. Scoffers to the contrary, I can accept the idea that God manifested angels <u>before</u> He manifested man."

"The word 'Angel' means 'Messenger", I pointed out. "And who can deny the possibility that God has delegated the execution of His Will to countless beings (angels) of far vaster wisdom and of far greater power than man has yet dreamed of."

"Violet, do you have a thought on that?" I asked my wife. Violet reflected a moment. Then commented, "It is natural for mortal man to try to make everything into his own image, or into a form less than his own. For example, we tend to think that the cosmic beings who come into our atmosphere in 'flying saucers' are humans ... mortals (or even monsters) from other planets. Yet in many cases, the real truth may be just the reverse -- they may be more than mortal beings. <u>They may be angels</u>!"

"Right," I agreed, "Biblical history plainly shows Angelic visits often made to this world. When seen, they were often mistaken for men. (See Gen. 19, etc.) I honestly believe that the times we now live in are so serious that Angelic ministry is now being manifested in our world, individually and Internationally."

This line of thought reminded me of a strange book I had been reading, and I felt impelled to go on talking. "The Book of Enoch (which is one of the 'lost' books of the Bible) has a passage that is quite revealing: 'And He will summon <u>all the host of the heavens, and all the holy ones above, and the host of God, the Cherubin, Seraphin, and Ophannin, and all the angels of power</u>, ... It then states that Seraphin are beings whose special duty is to serve in God's immediate presence. Cherubin form God's 'chariots', and Ophannin means 'wheels' like Ezekiel's 'wheel within a wheel '" I stopped speaking to give Violet a chance to say:

"Wonderful! That Book of Enoch passage and your explanation of that word, Ophannin, shed more light on the flying saucer mystery. Especially to those who see the Universe as intelligently directed by cosmic wisdom."

"And those," spoke up Anthony, "who see the universe as a soulless machine would probably scoff at the whole bit."

Luncheon concluded, the three of us left the restaurant and got into my car. As we transported Anthony through Hollywood traffic to his apartment, he drew from his briefcase a typed page containing more of the remarkable statements of the Master. We list them here as follows:

14. The minds of certain mortals are fused with divine direction, the expressions of which may appear of man's own doing. Modern evolution is but a directive from my Father who governs ALL.

15. If I were to return in peace no one would recognize me except my re-incarnate. The multitude will have to recognize me through a medium of might.

16. Reveal your experience to the elders and leaders of the Church. They will respond

and from that moment I will urge them , too.

17. Time is of little consequence now. As night approaches , day may never come - instead the light will pour forth from my Father's House.

18. I am the Truth, the Light , the ALL throughout the Universe.

19. Let all progress through me so that my vibrations may flow in ease - let this be the ANNUS MIRABILIS .

20. The Universal Link is growing - this is my sole consideration. GAUDEAMUS IGITUR .

21. Just as the tears fall from the Angel so will I fill the font for all to see.

22. There can be no real surprises - all must go according to plan without any exception whatsoever .

23. Of the documentary - ipsissima verba .

24. All is from me at all times and is being directed towards my units in a natural way. 25.

25. There will be a speeding up of the Universal vibrations from which there will be many outward happenings to many.

26. It is I who have created ALL - nothing is thrust upon me.

27. All questions are invited and will be answered.

CHAPTER 4
The Unveiling of 4 -D

On February 9 , 1964, in the early hours of the morning, I had a vision of a most remarkable being . As I lay quietly on my bed in the normal sleep state, suddenly my mental consciousness became sharp and clear , as if I were fully awake . Then before my inner eye appeared the dramatic features of a man. I was not shown the entire figure . Only the upper portion -- mainly the face and shoulders . The vision was in full colour, and impressed my total mind very deeply .

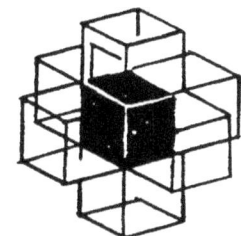

When first the vision flashed on, I was shown the profile of the being . His features were well defined, well formed, reflecting a tremendous inner strength and poise . Great calmness pervaded him. His hair, like spun gold , shone in an aura around his head.

Then this unusual personage turned slowly , so that I could see his face from a front view, and look directly into the eyes . The being did have a sparse beard, so that it resembled the one described by Richard Grave -- the one who is appearing to Mr. Grave consistently and giving him important instructions .

The vision I experienced lasted for only a few minutes, as far as I was able to ascertain, and while " on" , it gripped my full attention in the most remarkable manner.

No spoken words were transmitted to me throughout this experience , but I received the definite impression that this being wanted me to realize his reality ... to know he existed.

Before this experience , quite frankly , the whole business of a "Weeping Angel " picture in England and of some "Master " making regular appearances to a Mr. Grave, had little meaning for me. Now, suddenly it was all different. Now I was personally involved, at least to the extent of having seen a most unusual being in a totally unexpected vision . And although mine was only a vision , an image projected upon my inner consciousness , still it is my conviction that the being I saw was the same one who is now contacting Richard Grave in a more direct , objective way.

I have another strong conviction . It is this . You too, dear reader, are going to " see" this amazing being , even as I did, and you will then be greatly encouraged. But here it is well to keep in mind the thought that "Blessed are they who believe and have not seen. " Don't forget that the documented events of the "Weeping Angel " episode from 1961 through 1964 are extremely impressive evidence of the REALITY confronting us all .

Richard once asked the Cosmic Visitor , "Master, can you throw some light upon this question of others having seen you in a manner peculiar to them ? " The reply was,

"It is quite true; others have SEEN and HEARD ME in and through their own perceptive

powers. Everyone's power of perception depends upon whether they can clarify my direct vibration. To some it is difficult, to others like yourself it is easy by virtue of the receptive elements being stronger . This does not in any way mean that my power or vibration of my power is any less or greater throughout the whole operation either to you or to others -- . It simply means that to some, I GIVE A PARTICULAR FACULTY AMOUNTING TO CONTACT . "

After my own brief contact with " his" vibrations, I could not help but bring to mind more vividly the idea expressed to recently by Anthony Brooke during our visit . That is , the idea that the REAL world is soon to be manifested right under our very noses , so to speak -- and a Day of Reveltion is imminent. The mysterious "4th-Dimension" (whatever that is) is going to break through the hard exterior of our human minds!

The 4th- Dimension! I suddenly realized that I knew very little about it . But if a Cosmic Being was already manifesting himself visibly to Richard Grave, and if the same Cosmic Being has plans for an even greater demonstration by or before Christmas , 1967, I certainly ought to read up a little on the subject of the fourth dimension.

Have you ever wanted information on some topic and found yourself automatically drawn to the exact place where the knowledge you were seeking could be found ? Almost casually my hand skipped over the books in my library bookcase, and stopped, as if by some invisible direction, at one particular book. I took it from the bookcase. The title was, "A Primer of Higher Space" (The 4th - Dimension) by Claude Bragdon . I noted that it was written in 1913 and it most likely is out of print by now. I turned to the Foreword, where Mr. Bragdon had stated: "

The FOURTH DIMENSION of space is a memory- haunting phrase , so often heard, yet little understood... "

I for one could agree whole- heartedly with that observation! I knew almost nothing about "4- D" . The world you and I are aware of normally -- the sense world has 3 space dimensions , length, width and thickness.

Does a 4th- Dimension exist? Yes . The 3 Dimensions we know are included under the name of SPACE , and the 4th- Dimension is called TIME .

"One manner of conceiving the fourth dimension," wrote Mr. Claude Bragdon , "is as space changing in time... Time, in other words, is employed as though it were a dimension of space -- the FOURTH dimension. "

Now we are on the threshold of the big secret . If there is a fourth dimension, why not a fifth, a sixth, a seventh, etc. etc. ? Bragdon calls this dimensional area that apparently does exist beyond the 3- dimensional world, Hyperspace. " Hyperspace" , he wrote , "is mathematically REAL , and the master minds of science consider it to be PHYSICALLY POSSIBLE . (Einstein, Lord Kelvin, and others).

"Heaven is all about you, " Mr. Bragdon pointed out, "A city lying foursquare, clear as glass and filled with light . Here your real, your immortal selves, have their true home. This world of yours which seems so substantial is but a mutable and many- colored film

staining the bright radiance of this crystal heaven. Your lives are but tracings made by your immortal selves in this film world . How shall you learn the WAY to this heaven of light , the truth of this transcendent existence?"

The point is , since 1961, the Master has been making 4th- dimensional "entrances" upon the 3- dimensional experiences of Richard Grave. And.. ..<u>the veil is soon to be lifted for ALL .</u>

"<u>The lifting of the veil</u>, " states the Master , "means the lifting of that veil which prevents complete Universal sight - so allowing me fully to be perceived by ALL my Universal units. " Ready or not, one thing seems sure. The progressive unveiling of 4- D is going to dispel THE GREAT ILLUSION for many souls.

MORE STATEMENTS BY THE COSMIC MASTER
Important Dictations received by Richard Grave since 1961.

28. How happy I am with the progress being made throughout my Universe - the vibrations are very even.
29. Richard and I will reside for the time being near the waters at which point I appear in St.Annes -on-Sea. Here I will communicate my messages DE PROFUNDIS.
30. From these waters I will deliver many wonders .
31. I will deliver many truths VERBATIM ET LITTERATIM .
32. It is becoming necessary for me to interfere with the scientific devices of men and halt their progress .
33. My increased energy is circulating and may cause certain havoc which is within my arrangements . My energy is very even and everything smooth .
34. MY COMING AGAIN . THIS REFERS TO THE NEW VIBRATION AND DIVINE ENERGY THAT IS FEEDING MY UNIVERSE AT THIS MOMENT. I MEAN THE NEW AGE BY THE COMING AGAIN - I HAVE ALWAYS BEEN WITH THE UNIVERSE IN STAGE DEVELOPMENT WHICH CONSTITUTED MY FIRST SHOWING - NOW I AM IN THE ADVANCED AND FINAL SHOWING .
35. My work is increasing in obvious sequence - everything is running very smoothly .
36. I will intervene in many matters of science . I have not embarked on this procedure for the purpose of preventing the manifestation of any or all scientific development . I can HALT ALL MATTER at any time - without giving reason or warning . I am intent on bringing my earth plane to realize my very presence by practical means best recognizable by MAN.
37. A great many scientists are aware of an energy that is influencing their thesis .
38. All are regarding my influence as a challenge - none will stop to reason until I have created the means for them to appreciate FULLY that their program is limited in its entire objectivity .
39. You are meeting and making my link every day and my link is ready and waiting just to be joined together . My program is being brought forward.

CHAPTER 5
Tears -- in Hollywood

On Saturday morning, February 22, 1964 I received a telephone call from Anthony Brooke. He had exciting news for me. " This morning , around 6 A.M. , the photographic reproduction of the "Weeping Angel " picture - a copy at Katherine Hayward's studio in Hollywood , WEPT ! "

This was indeed news. Not only was the original Weeping Angel picture -- the one at Richard Grave's home in England -- capable of crying tears ; NOW the phenomenon had extended itself to North America !

"Katherine will be speaking about this new development on Sunday morning, " Anthony said. "If you attend the group meeting then, I am quite sure you will learn all of the details. I shall be there myself and I'd be happy to see you . The meeting is scheduled for 11:00 A.M. "

Katherine Hayward has known Liebie Pugh for many years and is a longtime friend of hers. In Autumn of 1959, Katherine came to California where she began to teach groups of people along lines of higher spiritual and mental development . She has spoken to millions of people in this country by means of numerous television and radio broadcasts on which she has appeared . In 1961, the Weeping Angel experiences of Richard Grave in England interested her, and she has been of real service in awakening America as to the facts confronting us.

Musing over this new turn of events, a recent statement by the Master flashed into my mind. " There will be many and more substantial manifestations to follow so that the prophecy of my coming may remain kindled."

On Sunday, February 23 I drove over to Katherine Hayward's studio apartment near Sunset Boulevard in Hollywood , California . She and Anthony both greeted me as I entered the room and sat down on a comfortable chair. Katherine's regular group had already assembled, and she stepped forward to give her talk .

"Very early Saturday morning, " she began, "a student of mine who had a copy of the Weeping Angel picture -- a photo taken of the original picture - called me about 6:00 A.M. , to say: 'Katherine, the picture is crying.'

"I asked her -- (we shall refer to her as Mrs. Z) to come over to my studio and bring the picture with her. When she arrived , she said: ' There it is Katherine for you to see - you see the tears ? ' I put my finger into the tears , there were, oh I suppose four or five drops

of water on the picture at that time, and I said: 'Yes, it's wet, Mrs. Z.'

"But my analytical mind would not let me believe that they were really there, although I also couldn't for one second believe that Mrs. Z could deceive me; but you see she had walked into the room with the picture already wet.

"In order that I myself might observe the weeping phenomenon under the severest test conditions, I took a dry cloth and wiped all of the moisture off the picture. Then I sat with her and talked and we were there for several hours. Meantime we had put the picture in front of the statue of Jesus we have here (pointing to a small statue quite near her).

"After our talk I went to see what had happened. The picture was perfectly dry. This time with Mrs. Z quite close I held it and within seconds <u>it began to cry again and continued to do so.</u> This time I had no doubt."

Katherine Hayward then continued her special talk. I shall try to paraphrase her words and thoughts, as accurately as is possible from the few brief notes I made as she spoke.

"I don't want to give you the impression that phenomena of this kind is new to me and I have always said, 'So what - the picture cried - but that doesn't for one moment portray to me that the promises made are going to be fulfilled.' But there is more to this today than just that which I have told you.

"I am a very busy person and there is a great deal to be done in this studio that only I am able to do. This morning I wondered if, not having any <u>real</u> conviction about this and about the prophecies given through Richard, I shouldn't pass on to somebody else the questions I get by letter and otherwise here in America, such as: 'Have you seen the picture cry?' I thought that if I could only say 'Yes', it would impress the people who need this kind of thing to awaken them.

"This morning, as I hadn't seen it for myself, I decided to write to Liebie and say: 'Liebie, look - appoint someone else. Talk to the Visitor and ask him if it would not be better for someone else to take this on.' <u>And this morning Mrs. Z arrived.</u> ("This" morning refers to Saturday.)

"Of course we know that the pattern of life is already set and it was so arranged.

"There was another very unusual thing. I do not see people on Saturday mornings, but I did see Mrs. Z this morning, also Anthony Brooke. He saw the wet too, but he didn't see it come from the dry. But he saw it wet and he knows enough about me to know <u>it really was wet and it came there of its own accord.</u>

"This phenomenon of the Weeping Angel has a purpose. It is to attract attention of humanity to that which is to take place in our world soon, according to the words of the Being who has been appearing to Richard Grave in England. A changeover is predicted by this Being. He has stated that there will be many who will receive their own confirmation of this.

"The most essential thing now, is that we learn to know more about ourselves. You need not GO anywhere. Only turn inward in stillness and discover THAT about yourself

which will give you real satisfaction. The truth is, there is MORE to you than you now know. Ask yourself: What can I do to learn more about myself? This is how you prepare the way for the New World.

"Since 1959 when I first came to California, I have been teaching that it is exceedingly important and useful and practical for us to change our own body habits so as to be better able to function in the NEW VIBRATIONS.

"In the New Vibrations," Katherine said, "you know deep within you, that you are more than you perceive through your five senses. Man is Divine - nothing else but Divine -

"God is here seeing the world through your eyes."

The talk thus concluded, there followed a friendly "get acquainted" period in which members of the group chatted freely with each other. Several persons clustered around Katherine Hayward, asking her questions and telling her how much they enjoyed this talk. I took the opportunity to inquire about Mrs. Z. Had she attended this morning's meeting?

Unfortunately she had not. Katherine explained that Mrs. Z was a deeply sensitive woman and that the experience of seeing the Angel weeping had moved her profoundly, and so she had decided to remain "incognito"

You perhaps are wondering at this point. Do I personally believe that a manifestation of the Weeping Angel phenomenon really took place in Hollywood as we have described? My reply is - yes. I have no reason to doubt for a second the inherent honesty, truthfulness and spiritual integrity of any of these three witnesses to the manifestation.

An Angel in a picture did <u>weep</u> -- in Hollywood.

CHAPTER 6

The Prediction

<u>On Friday , May 3 , 1963</u> , a newspaper columnist, Helen Derek, wrote an exceptionally clear and vivid account of the "Weeping Angel " story in her column, "Girl About Town" . The article appeared in the "Reading and Berkshire Chronicle ".

In order that you may know the story from her point of view, as well as mine, I will here present important excerpts from Helen Derek's splendid article. Doubtless it will give you many valuable details which I , perhaps , may have overlooked in my telling of this incredible but tremendously VITAL story .

'TEARS ' THAT FLOW FROM THE VICTORIAN PRINT

By Helen Derek

"One of the strangest public meetings I have ever attended was in Reading last week. Its full importance is hard to define. I don't think it is my task to try to do so. I'll tell you the facts , leave you to think about them on your own. If Richard Grave's story rings true, doubtless you will want to know more, wish to investigate personally .

"Mr. Grave, a 34-years -old property dealer , who lives in Lancashire, came to Reading at the invitation of the A.W.R.E. Society for Psychic Research, to talk about the remarkable picture in his possession which, apparently , shows an angel weeping real tears . Your immediate reaction to this may be perhaps to sneer . But bear in mind that HUNDREDS have witnessed the 'weeping ' , that top representatives of the churches have accepted the phenomenon as genuine , that national newspapermen who went to scoff, left <u>convinced</u>...

"The 'Weeping Angel of Worthing ' was , not unnaturally , 'hot news' of the day , locally ; then also nationally , as television cameras went down to Worthing to try to record the strange phenomenon . It was made clear to viewers by the I.T.V. spokesman that he had indeed seen the ' tears ' fall from the face of the Angel . Unnecessary to add, incidentally , that there was no secreted phial , aid, or whatever with which Mr. Grave could have faked the happening.

"The Reading audience, spellbound, were told by Mr. Grave, in his straightforward , matter- of-fact way , how the "Weeping Angel' <u>heralded an event of much greater significance</u> . For the figure that had at first claimed him , which appeared only to him, was soon to make regular visitations to his house in Worthing .

(The article now quotes Richard directly , in his own words .)

'It all started with those first glimpses , then built up so that I could see and talk to a man I called "Master". The bearded visitor , dressed in coarse robes with a red outer garment ,

appears suddenly , and when I can see him he is as solid and real as the next man. I last saw and spoke to him at midday today . The Master has told me he is the Truth, the Light , the ALL throughout the Universe.

"The figure has also told Richard Grave that he (the Master) will intervene in many matters of science: 'A great many scientists are aware of an energy that is influencing their theses . My coming- again refers to the new vibration , and divine energy that is feeding my universe at this moment..

* * * * * * * * *

I have purposely under- scored several sentences in the article you have just read. Let us look more closely at those sentences, for they may give us greater " insight " regarding the real significance of the "Weeping Angel " phenomenon .

" ... heralded an event of much greater significance ."

This event concerns the great universal revelation which the Supernormal Being promises to make

In the exact words of the Master to Richard , here is how this tremendous prediction was stated:

"Have no thought towards the seeming confusion of others around you ALL is in MY Universal Plan - although the time is opportune for a physical UNIVERSAL LINK to be formed among those inspired it must be remembered that ALL must walk only in the light that reflects TRUTH to them. No man can know the DAY or HOUR when MY great Universal Revelation will be enacted, however , I must repeat - BY THE FIRST SECOND OF THE FIRST HOUR OF CHRISTMAS MORNING I WILL HAVE RE - VEALED MYSELF TO THE UNIVERSE through the medium OF NUCLEAR EVOLUTION - This is my PLAN which is absolute. There will be many who will receive their own confirmation and who will be moved to contact you. ALL IS WELL. "

The other sentence I have underscored is ,

"This will be done through the medium of nuclear evolution."

Marvelous. But what does "nuclear evolution" mean? That is the big key to the whole thing . The entire universal revelation must hinge upon this idea, this process. Are we humans able to grasp this ? Can we understand this new process -- nuclear evolution -- and how to interpret it ? To this question I answer: YES . Some of us are already sensing the secret of this throbbing God-power - that dwells in the atom.

Between now and 2000, a brand new idea will burst upon the waiting consciousness of all of us. The idea will concern itself with the unlocking of the divinity of the atoms of which you are constructed. It will emphasize motive. Not the limited motive of mere

survival. But the unlimited motive of spiritual evolution of the consciousness within the NUCLEUS of the atom.. <u>This will be a part of the great Universal Revelation.</u>

"Only my WHOLE SELF will be kept invisible," said the Master to Richard, "until THE DAY - until then many WILL see aspects of ME in many forms - ALL of which are throughout the fulness of me."

Frequently, people ask Richard Grave why it was that the Master selected him to work through, rather than someone else.

"That's something I've wondered, of course," Richard says. " The Master said I was an instrument he'd been using a long time, unknown to me. I was an ordinary chap with an ordinary sort of a job.

"When all began with the picture and so on, I thought I was going mad. So much has happened since, in which other people all over the country have proved for themselves that the Master must be a REAL person with very REAL intentions, that my peace of mind has returned. <u>And I am convinced of all that is to come.</u> "

It is my inner conviction, as I write this, that the Master very definitely IS real and so are his intentions. His revelation of the Real is even NOW beginning to burst in upon the aware minds of those in the vanguard of earth's humanity. I too, am convinced of ALL THAT IS TO COME.

MORE STATEMENTS BY THE MASTER

40.   40. One evening in the half-light of the kitchen Richard described how the Master appeared and his whole self seemed to be alight with a sharp but pleasing light. Richard went on - "When he had finished talking to me, he placed his right arm around me, raised me and said, 'Walk to the door with me,' and we both walked to the front door. The Master opened the hall door whilst I opened the front door and there stood a host of people thronging my path and garden. The Master stepped out among them and then he and the group disappeared together.

41. The description of my energies in the documentary is perfect.

42. I do NOT build and rebuild my physical form when I appear to my medium - I am always present in full form.

43. My WHOLE SELF is never divided.

44. I am most active on all planes at this moment and many things will become evident through the medium of others both on and off my link - all subjects are on my link by degree - some being on my level of vibration - My Universal Link is satisfactory.

45. During the time of the move Richard asked - "Master, why have there been fewer visits from you over the past two weeks?" Reply: Whether I visit you once or twice or not at all in any day has no bearing on the progress being made and my program. I could remain with you always if I so desired - the contact is made - now it remains only for me to deliver messages as and when they are required by me to my earth units so named by me.

46. Many matters are being brought now to the notice of all on my link . I am happy with my Universal arrangements - you too are progressing nicely my son 9 try to remain as quiet as possible over the next few days so that you may respond more deeply to my influences. Keep an eye on the waters from where my wonders will come. (The Master disappeared with the smile of an angel) .

47. The day after my arrival at St. Annes , Richard brought the following message. At 11:05 P.M. last evening a major universal phase was completed . My greater force was released - the polarization of my planets was completed . I require the Park and Sea areas for the conducting of my universal energy. All is being directed from St.Annes at this moment and other units from the South will be required to settle within my area at very short notice. Many major developments must be evident on completion in the course of this earth year. The whole of my program is even. Vibrations are increasing and my Universe is being impregnated.

CHAPTER 7
Disaster or... Revelation?

I have reserved this final chapter of our Monograph for a very serious discussion . Here you and I will consider one of the messages received by Richard from the Master , which deals with the specific event which is to " signal " the manifestation of the Great Universal Revelation. "

By the time the first primrose breaks through again , " said the Master on November 13, 1961, " the present Universal phase will have been completed and the LAST phase before THE DAY will have begun .

"A Major World Conflict will herald the LAST stages of the Universal progress. In the meantime general world conditions will show evidence of a leading up to the introduction of a NUCLEAR DEVICE that will bring about the final human level episode . The major conflict I speak of will bebetween nations and it will be most sudden."

Oh, oh. What have we here? Disaster for all of us ? You know as well as I that a Major World Conflict 10 World War III -- would wreak frightful havoc on the entire race of humanity .

But wait. Read on. Read what Liebie Pugh wrote concerning this most critical point in the Master's prediction . I quote: "In relation to this message I should add that the Master told Richard in the early months of his visits, that, on the day when he will reveal himself to the Universe, the course of events will be as follows:

"A human press- button device will be used and, simultaneously with the pressing of the button - <u>INSTEAD OF DISASTER - THE UNIVERSAL REVELATION WILL OCCUR .</u>

"On first reading of this messagethe reference to the World Conflict may startle some - but taken together with the earlier statement there is only glorious reassurance in this renewed and clear reference to the final human level episode which is the SIGNAL for the Great Revelation.

"Richard and I feel it will bring inspiration to many to know that by the early Spring we shall have entered the LAST phase - leading to the Day of REVELATION. For this reason I am having this message typed in order to share it with all who have so far followed these great events most closely .

"It has come to my notice that a few of those reading this message, mistakenly think that the breaking of the first primrose is to be the signal for the Great Revelation. This is NOT the case. All that is stated is that, at the time of the primrose the last phase LEADING TO THE DAY will have begun and there is no reference to the duration of the last phase."

In another newsletter, Liebie Pugh summarizes the amazing sequence of events that have taken place to date:

"He (the Cosmic Being) first drew human attention to his presence and activity by means of various phenomena such as the weeping of the Angel in a picture in Worthing. A full account of these signs has been given in a <u>Documentary</u> which he wished me to write and which is now available to all, so no more need be said of these signs here.

"<u>In 1953</u>, Katherine Hayward was brought into contact with me, and through her great mediumship I was informed that she was to be instrumental in bringing about a manifestation of the REAL WORLD to humanity in this generation, and that the SIGN of this manifestation would be that it was <u>beyond question and beyond doubt.</u> It was made plain that I had a part to play in this operation. Among other things I was given through Katherine Hayward the instruction to model a new head of 'The Master'. I use here the <u>name</u> which was used at the time the instruction was given. This was done.

"It has since been named 'Limitless Love', and photographs of it have been widely circulated and deeply appreciated. When in 1961, several years after this model was made, this super-normal visitor appeared to Richard Grave, I showed him this photograph and he was overwhelmed by it, and declared it to be an exact likeness of the one who was visiting him. In addition to this, the visitor asked me to emphasize Richard's recognition of it as a complete portrayal of himself, in the Documentary which is titled: "NOTHING ELSE MATTERS'. So the sequence of events was as follows:

> 1953 Katherine Hayward joined forces with me, and, through her, information was given of the manifestation of the Real World, which was coming in our time.
>
> 1957-8 I was instructed to model a new head of the Master and did so.
>
> 1961 The Master appeared in solid form to Richard Grave who, the moment he saw the photograph of the head, modelled several years earlier, identified it with his visitor.

Now, dear reader, if we add to these facts an additional fact 13 · namely, that the Supernormal Visitor has appeared personally and objectively more than 6,000 times to Richard Grave, and is still continuing to do so -- we cannot help but conclude that something of tremendous significance must be happening.

But here is something even more significant. A Universal Linking process is going on

> * Early Spring of 1962. This was the time, you will recall, when the Great Conjunction of seven planets in the sign of Aquarius, occurred in the heavens. A most auspicious event, esoterically and spiritually.

now -- and it is not limited to this planet. "THE DIVINE LINKING IS PROGRESSING FAR BEYOND THE EARTH."

I have honestly tried, in this Monograph, not to "sweeten the truth" for you. I have simply reported the facts as they now stand. Quite frankly, I would never have written this report had not "he" -- the Master, the visitor, the Cosmic Being in his infinite compassion and strength, made himself known to me inwardly. If this little writing I have done, turns out to be useful to that great Being in the outworking of his PLAN, then it will in - deed have been worth the effort.

For in his universal love, that Being is embracing YOU and all of the other splendid, spiritually evolved and evolving souls who are loyal to the higher principles of Love, Power and Wisdom.

Motive is supremely important. I am loyal to the Being I have described in this monograph, because I respect his motive. It is Godlike. It is universal. "ALL IS WITHIN MY PLAN" he is telling us. Fear not. "ALL IS WELL". He is responsible for the phenomenon of the "Weeping Angel" which is destined to awaken millions of New-Age individuals, into the inevitable and evolutionary awareness of the REAL ... the God in all of us.

My friend, it has been wonderful visiting with you. We've shared much together, yet I feel it is only the beginning of adventures to come. Till then, God bless you! Look up -- with me -- to the soon- coming "moment of truth" when, instead of disaster - <u>THE UNIVERSAL REVELATION WILL OCCUR! THE END AND THE BEGINNING!</u>

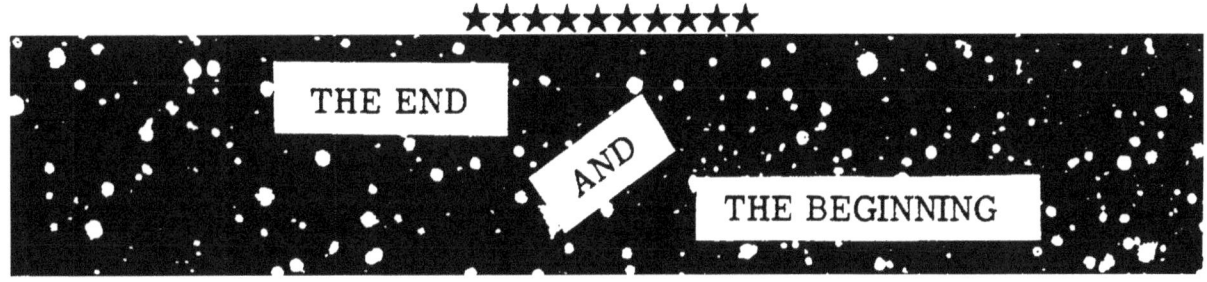

ADDITIONAL TESTIMONY

Mr. Michael X. Barton
5949 Gregory Avenue
Los Angeles, Calif. 90038

Dear Michael:

In regards to your phone call requesting a written description of what occurred at the Long Beach Cosmic Star Center on June 7th, 1964, pertaining to the "Weeping Angel Picture".

Indeed the picture did weep. After arriving at the office on the above mentioned date, I proceeded to rearrange the platform for the next speaker. Having already been informed of your having left your lecture notes and the Weeping Angel Picture on the platform after your lecture here, I immediately set out to gather up those items for you. When I first noticed the picture it was on the chair directly behind the rostrum. Upon reaching for it I saw <u>the picture had the most beautiful glow</u> coming from and around it -- the brightest part of the glow being from the upper left corner. <u>The whole picture was bathed in a purple radiance</u>. Upon inspecting this unique phenomenon I noticed that the Weeping Angel picture was quite <u>wet</u> at the bottom part of the frame, a good ½ of the water resting on the lower end of the frame.

Where the large single tear shows in the picture, was a large, lone, perfect tear. Immediately I put my finger in this, smeared it. It was most assuredly <u>water</u>. I wiped the picture dry.

After gathering up your notes, with the picture placed on top of all this, I left the stage, noticing while leaving the area that the purple radiance around the picture decreased. As I proceeded to the outer office the entire phenomenon had completely disappeared.

To you Michael I say this - When looking at the tears on this picture, and wiping them away, I had the feeling that "The Weeping Angel" was weeping for all humanity. Words could not be written to express the feeling or vibrations that went through me and the Star Center at that particular moment. I only wish that you and Violet, and everyone could have seen this strange picture. It was indeed wonderful to say the least. Perhaps it will weep again here for us all to behold. One never knows.

The volume: "The Weeping Angel Prediction" is indeed a great achievement in the literary field. We here in Long Beach at the Center wish you the best of luck.

Sincerely,

Victoria E. Petrie

No Earthly Explanation...
Hit by a car, my guardian angel saved my life.

Most theologians accept the fact that we all have at least one guardian angel who protects us against harm. Guardian angels have been known to watch over the sick, guide the helpless out of potentially harmful situations, and, in general, watch over us when danger is near.

There are many recorded instances where guardian angels have proven time after time, that they can be called upon to be "good samaritans," given the opportunity. The following TRUE story was submitted by Barbara Leeds, an artist and song writer who lives and works in New York City. Her account quite clearly illustrates the fact that we never have to walk alone.

* * *

Anyone whose ever been to Manhattan, can tell you that you'd better look both ways before stepping off the curb. If you don't keep an eye out for oncoming traffic, chances are, you are going to get "clobbered". as I did several years ago.

In the "Big Apple," cabs and cars don't come to an immediate halt like in most other cities. When a pedestrian decides to walk out into the street, it's every man, woman and child for themselves.

I had just been to see a music publisher on 57th Street about getting one or two of my songs recorded. The publisher liked my most recent tunes and offered words of encouragement. I guess, looking back now on what happened, that I must have felt a bit "light headed," as I dashed across Madison Avenue on my way to my next appointment.

No doubt, the driver of the stationwagon that plowed into me had other things on his mind, and wasn't about to slow down for anyone as he rounded the corner.

I didn't have time to think, everything happened so fast. I saw the vehicle coming, but couldn't back up onto the sidewalk in time. I should have been killed, he was driving so fast. Instead, at the last second, I felt a hand grab me by the seat of my pants and the next thing I knew, I was being lifted into the air and was let down lightly on the hood of the speeding station wagon. The vehicle was traveling so fast, that it took the driver a half a block to come to a complete stop. When he got out of the car to see if he had killed me, there I was, sitting cross

Barbara Leeds holds drawing of angel.

legged on the hood without a scratch. There wasn't a black and blue mark anywhere on my body. And most important of all, there was no one around who could have been responsible for lifting me into the air and depositing me so carefully back down, and in a sitting position to boot.

The fact that I know I have an "invisible friend" around me at all times, doesn't worry me. The truth is, I'm happy to know that there's someone - somewhere "out there" - who is willing to give me a helping hand when I need it the most.

* * *

We invite readers who have had an experience involving an angel to share their personal encounter with our many readers. We will pay $5 for each story we use, but we do retain the right to edit your story as we see fit. Send your experience to INNER LIGHT, Box 753, New Brunswick, New Jersey 08903. If you are interested in reading further accounts of this type we suggest the book ANGELS OF THE LORD by Arthur Crockett. An ad for this exciting volume appears on the opposite page.

REPRINTED FROM INNER LIGHT ISSUE NUMBER ONE

www.ingramcontent.com/pod-product-compliance
Lightning Source LLC
Chambersburg PA
CBHW080554170426

43195CB00016B/2788